"十一五"期间国家重点图书出版规划项目

中国国家汉办重点规划教材

age edition

5A

MONKEY KING CHINESE

美猴王汉语

(少儿)

编者：刘富华　王巍　周芮安

翻译：邵壮

北京语言大学出版社
BEIJING LANGUAGE AND CULTURE
UNIVERSITY PRESS

THE MONKEY KING

Sun Wukong, the Handsome Monkey King, is the hero of the Chinese literary classic *Journey to the West* (Wu Cheng'en, the Ming Dynasty). This novel was based on a true story of a famous Chinese monk, Xuan Zang (602 ~ 664). After years of trials and tribulations, he traveled on foot to what is today India, the birthplace of Buddhism, to seek for the Sutra, the Buddhist holy book. Finally he got the sutras and returned to China, or the Great Tang as was called at that time. He translated the sutras into Chinese, thus making contribution to the development of Buddhism in China.

In this novel, Buddha arranged for a monkey to become the monk's disciple and escort him, to ensure that he makes it to the west to get the sutras. The monkey called Sun Wukong, made the adventurous journey with Tangseng (the master), the other two disciples—Zhubajie (the pig-man) and Shaheshang (the monk) and Bailongma(the horse).

Sun Wukong was born out of a rock and fertilized by the grace of Heaven. In the Water Curtain Cave in the Mountain of Flower and Fruit, he was the King of the monkeys. Being extremely smart and capable, he learned all the magic tricks and kungfu from a Taoist master. He can transform himself into seventy-two different images such as a tree, a bird, a beast of prey or a bug as small as a mosquito so as to sneak into an enemy's belly to fight him or her inside out. Using clouds as a vehicle he can travel 108,000 *li* by a single somersault. The handsome Monkey King excelled in supernatural powers, defied hardships and dangers, and killed monsters. He protected his master Xuan Zang to overcome the eighty-one difficulties in fourteen years of the journey, and finally attained the Buddhist scriptures.

The Monkey King who is omnipotent, brave and winsome, is deeply beloved by Chinese children and adults alike even up till now.

To Teachers

Monkey King Chinese (school-age edition) is a series of elementary Chinese language primers for primary school children from the 1st year to the 3rd year in English-speaking countries. This series of textbooks is divided into three levels according to the year rank. Each level consists of two volumes, A and B. There are altogether six volumes and a total vocabulary of 251 words in the three levels.

Owing to a full understanding on the dispositions and learning habits of primary school pupils aged from seven to ten in English-speaking countries, the editors have chosen topics which appeal to children and at the same time decrease difficulties of the contents to add more fun in the learning process. The aim of this series of textbooks is to give the children a preliminary understanding of the Chinese language through fun games and lay a good foundation for future systematic study.

The style and content arrangement of the textbooks are in accordance with the principle of progressing in an orderly and step-by-step way. Some topics among the three levels may be repeated but their difficulty is increased gradually. Words are the focus of the first level; phrases are the focus of the second level; and sentences the third level. The style and content arrangement of each level are as follows:

Level One: Words are the foundation, supplemented by Pinyin, nursery rhymes, handicrafts, and exercises, among which Pinyin are mainly single finals and tones.

Level Two: Word groups and phrases are the foundation, supplemented by Pinyin, nursery rhymes, handicrafts, and exercises, among which Pinyin are compound spellings of initials and finals.

Level Three: Short sentences are the foundation, supplemented by nursery rhymes, Chinese characters coloring tasks, words and expressions for everyday use, handicrafts, and exercises. Compared with the first two levels, Level Three has some simple Chinese characters, words and expressions for everyday use, and functions as a transition for regular Chinese language education.

Some suggestions to teachers:

1. Teacher leads the reading of words and expressions, sentences, nursery rhymes of each lesson using vocabulary cards, Pinyin cards, and CD.

2. Teacher can give some necessary explanations to the Chinese characters, handicrafts and the exercises. Then allow the children to freely express

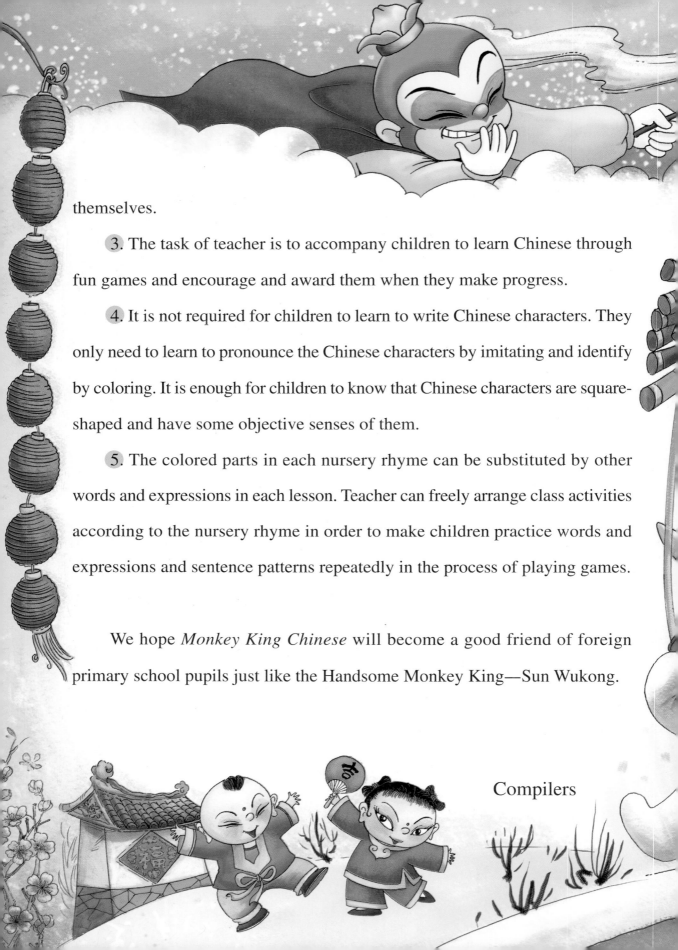

themselves.

3. The task of teacher is to accompany children to learn Chinese through fun games and encourage and award them when they make progress.

4. It is not required for children to learn to write Chinese characters. They only need to learn to pronounce the Chinese characters by imitating and identify by coloring. It is enough for children to know that Chinese characters are square-shaped and have some objective senses of them.

5. The colored parts in each nursery rhyme can be substituted by other words and expressions in each lesson. Teacher can freely arrange class activities according to the nursery rhyme in order to make children practice words and expressions and sentence patterns repeatedly in the process of playing games.

We hope *Monkey King Chinese* will become a good friend of foreign primary school pupils just like the Handsome Monkey King—Sun Wukong.

Compilers

Contents

FRIEND'S HOUSE

1. Say it.

chuānglián 窗帘

dēnglong 灯笼

chuānghu 窗户

mén 门

huāpíng 花瓶

Cháhú zhēn piàoliang. 茶壶真漂亮。

cháhú 茶壶

...... zhēn piàoliang.
...... 真 漂亮。 How beautiful...is/are!

2. Chant it.

Zhè shì wǒ de jiā,

Jiā li zhēn piàoliang.

Shénme zuì piàoliang?

Cháhú zuì piàoliang.

This is my house,

How beautiful my house is!

What is the most beautiful inside?

The teapot is the most beautiful.

3. Color it.

4. Try it.

Nǐ hǎo.
你好。

Nǐ hǎo.
你好。

Hello.   Hello.

5. Do it.

Make a toy tiger out of an eggshell.

1

6. Exercises.

(1) Listen, circle and draw.

(2) Join the red dots and see what it would be.

Zhēn piàoliang.
真 漂 亮 。

(3) Join the dots and read.

① Chuānglián zhēn piàoliang.

② Huāpíng zhēn piàoliang.

③ Cháhú zhēn piàoliang.

④ Mén zhēn piàoliang.

LOVELY KITCHEN

1. Say it.

Pánzi duō.
盘子 多。

Wǎn shǎo.
碗 少。

pánzi
盘子

wǎn
碗

chāzi
叉子

kuàizi
筷子

dāozi
刀子

sháozi
勺子

...... duō.
⋯⋯ 多。 There are many...

...... shǎo.
⋯⋯ 少。 There are few...

2. Sing it.

Suàn Yi Suàn
算一算

作曲：汤韵

Allegro

Yí ge duō, yí ge shǎo,

shí ge pán zi, sān ge sháo.

Suàn yi suàn, shǎo jǐ ge?

Shǎo qī ge ya shǎo qī ge.

Zhēn shì cōngming de hǎo bǎobao.

One kind is large in number, the other kind is small in number.

There are ten dishes and three spoons.

Figure out how many spoons are short?

Seven spoons are short.

How clever and lovely the child is!

3. Color it. 永

4. Try it.

Bú   kèqi.

不 客 气。

Xièxie.

谢谢。

Thanks.   You are welcome.

5. Do it.

Paper-cut: Cut a small fork.

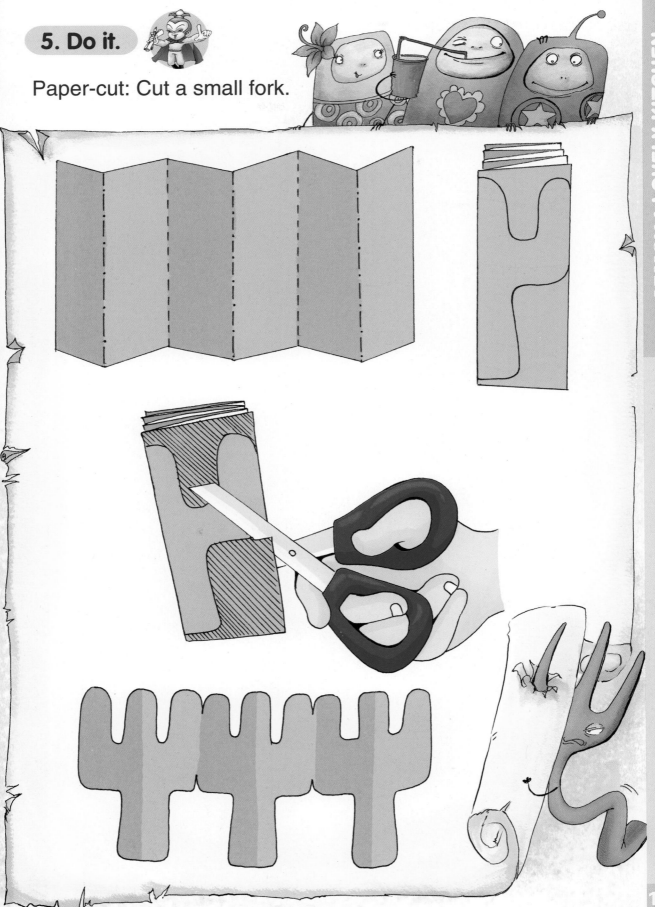

6. Exercises.

(1) Learn to draw and join the dots.

pánzi
wǎn
dāozi
sháozi

(2) Look and stick.

pánzi

chāzi

kuàizi

sháozi

dāozi

(3) Look and tick.

	duō 多	shǎo 少
wǎn 碗		
pánzi 盘子		
kuàizi 筷子		
chāzi 叉子		

Lesson 3

CHINESE FOOD

1. Say it.

Zhè shì kǎoyā.
这 是 烤鸭。

kǎoyā
烤鸭

chūnjuǎn
春卷

bǐng
饼

jiǎozi
饺子

chǎofàn
炒饭

chǎomiàn
炒面

Zhè shì ……
这 是…… This is.../These are...

14

2. Chant it.

Kàn yi kàn, cāi yi cāi,

Zhè shì shénme cài?

Zhè shì chūnjuǎn,

Zhè shì chūnjuǎn,

Zhè shì hǎochī de Zhōngguó cài,

Have a look at it, then make a guess.

What dish is it?

This is spring roll.

This is spring roll.

This is a delicious Chinese dish.

3. Color it.

4. Try it.

Duìbuqǐ.
对不起。

Méi guānxi.
没关系。

Sorry. It doesn't matter.

5. Do it.

Make a Chinese food menu.

①

 ②

③

④

Chinese Food

kǎoyā

chǎofàn

jiǎozi

Color the foods in supplementary page I .

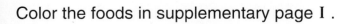

6. Exercises.

(1) Read and stick.

chǎofàn

chǎomiàn

chūnjuǎn

bǐng

(2) Look, number and join the dots.

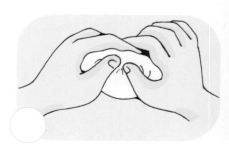

(3) Read and choose  or 😞.

Zhè shì chǎofàn.
这 是 炒饭。

Zhè shì kǎoyā.
这 是 烤鸭。

Zhè shì bǐng.
这 是 饼。

Zhè shì chūnjuǎn.
这 是 春卷。

EXCURSION

1. Say it.

Wǒmen pá shān.
我们爬山。

pá shān
爬山

chàng gē
唱歌

pǎo bù
跑步

qí chē
骑车

tiào wǔ
跳舞

huá chuán
划船

Wǒmen ......
我们…… We...

2. Sing it.

Tiān Lán Lán

天蓝蓝

作曲：汤韵

Allegro

Xīng qī tiān ya tiān lán lán,

wǒ men yì qǐ chū qù wánr.

Qù pá shān ya qù huá chuán,

liǎn dàn biàn chéng xiǎo huā liǎn.

Today is Sunday, the sky is blue,

Let's go out to play.

Go climbing, go boating,

And the little faces become dirty.

3. Color it.

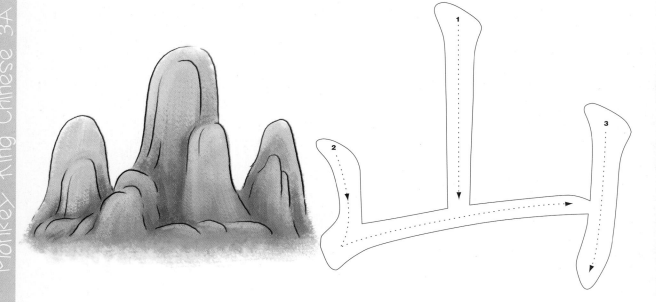

4. Try it.

Huānyíng.
欢迎。

Welcome.

Monkey King Chinese 3A

5. Do it.

Make a "squirrel litter".

Cut the squirrel out from supplementary page **II**.

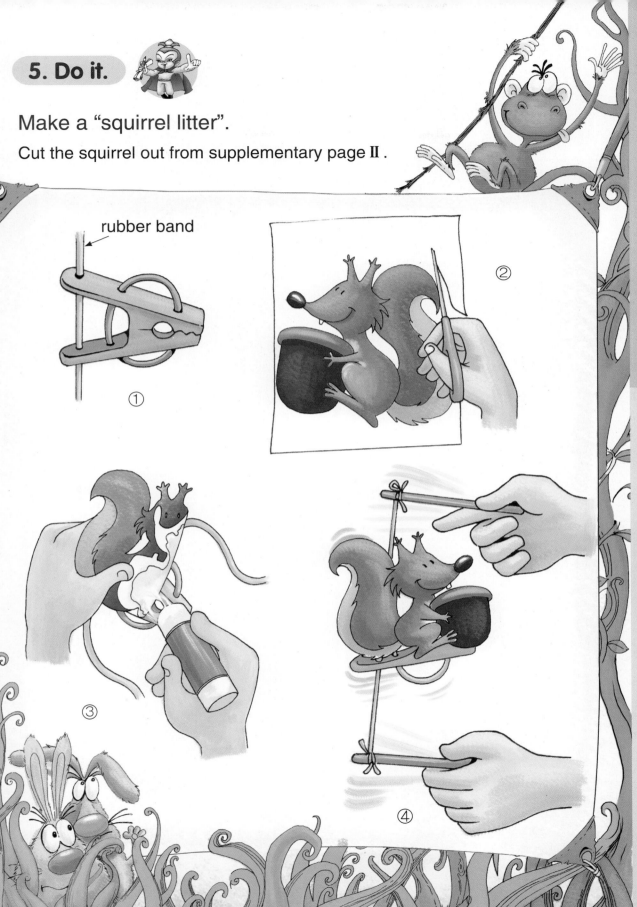

rubber band

① ② ③ ④

6. Exercises.

(1) Listen and write down the number for each picture.

○   ○   ○   ○

(2) Find out and say.

What are they going to do?

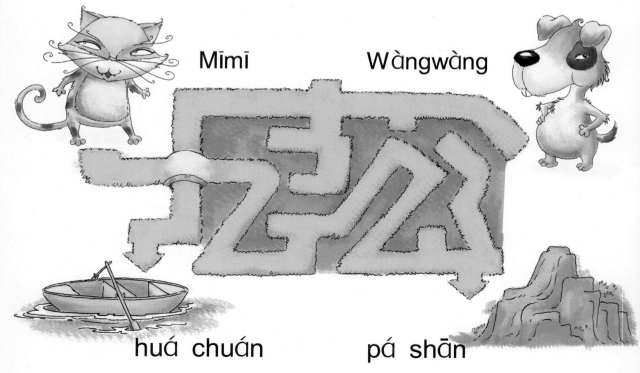

Mīmī   Wàngwàng

huá chuán   pá shān

(3) Look and say.

Wǒmen ······
我们 ······

IN THE ORCHARD

1. Say it.

căoméi
草莓

mángguǒ
芒果

pútao
葡萄

Wǒ xǐhuan pútao.
我 喜欢 葡萄。

bōluó
菠萝

níngméng
柠檬

Wǒ xǐhuan ……
我 喜欢…… I like...

2. Chant it.

Guǒyuán li, shuǐguǒ duō.

Wǒmen yìqǐ zhāi shuǐguǒ.

Wǒ xǐhuan cǎoméi,

Wǒ xǐhuan bōluó,

Zhāi shuǐguǒ, lè hēhē.

In the orchard there are many kinds of fruits.

Let's pick fruits together.

I like strawberry.

I like pineapple.

Picking fruits is cheerful and fun.

3. Color it.

4. Try it.

Qǐng jìn.
请 进。

Come in, please.

5. Do it.

Cut and stick a fruit basket.

Color the fruits and the fruit basket in supplementary page II.

6. Exercises.

(1) Color and match.

níngméng   **bōluó**   **pútao**   **cǎoméi**

(2) Count, join the dots and write.

mángguǒ _____

(3) Look and write.

What fruits do they like?

IN THE FARM

1. Say it.

Mǎ yǒu wěiba.
马 有 尾 巴。

wěiba
尾 巴

zhū
猪

mǎ
马

dùzi
肚 子

bízi
鼻 子

gǒu
狗

ěrduo
耳 朵

niú
牛

tùzi
兔 子

yǎnjing
眼 睛

...... yǒu ......
......有...... ...has/have...

2. Sing it.

Kàn Yi Kàn

看一看

作曲：汤韵

Allegro

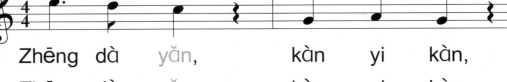

Zhēng dà yǎn, kàn yi kàn,
Zhēng dà yǎn, kàn yi kàn,

shén me cháng ya shén me duǎn?
shén me dà ya shén me xiǎo?

Shuí de wěi ba cháng? Mǎ de wěi ba cháng.
Shuí de yǎn jing dà? Niú de yǎn jing dà.

Shuí de wěi ba duǎn? Tù zi wěi ba duǎn.
Shuí de yǎn jing xiǎo? Zhū de yǎn jing xiǎo.

Open the eyes wide and take a look.

Whose tail is longer?

The horse's tail is longer.

Whose tail is shorter?

The rabbit's tail is shorter.

Whose eyes are bigger?

The cow's eyes are bigger.

Whose eyes are smaller?

The pig's eyes are smaller.

3. Color it.

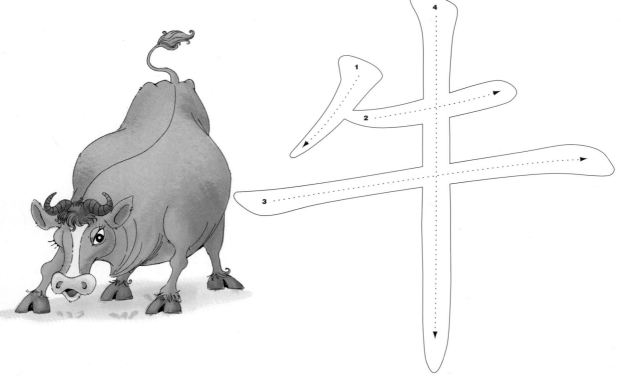

4. Try it.

Zàijiàn.
再见。

Zàijiàn.
再见。

Goodbye. Goodbye.

5. Do it.

Learn to draw a single-stroke drawing.

6. Exercises.

(1) Look and stick.

zhū

gǒu

māo

niú

(2) Look, join the dots and find out the differences.

tùzi

(3) Look and match.

Mǎ yǒu bízi.
马 有 鼻子。

Mǎ yǒu yǎnjing.
马 有 眼睛。

Mǎ yǒu wěiba.
马 有 尾巴。

Mǎ yǒu dùzi.
马 有 肚子。

茶壶

窗帘

爬山

叉子

勺子

跳舞

牛

葡萄

烤鸭

盘子

划船

菠萝

饺子

花瓶

碗

马

草莓

炒饭

筷子

窗户

狗

骑车

灯笼

猪

WORD LIST

Monkey King Chinese 3A

B

| 饼 | bǐng | pancake | 3 |
| 菠萝 | bōluó | pineapple | 5 |

C

草莓	cǎoméi	strawberry	5
叉子	chāzi	fork	2
茶壶	cháhú	teapot	1
唱歌	chàng gē	sing	4
炒饭	chǎofàn	fried rice	3
炒面	chǎomiàn	fried noodles	3
窗户	chuānghu	window	1
窗帘	chuānglián	curtain	1
春卷	chūnjuǎn	spring roll	3

D

| 刀子 | dāozi | knife | 2 |
| 灯笼 | dēnglong | lantern | 1 |

| 肚子 | dùzi | belly | 6 |
| 多 | duō | many | 2 |

G

| 狗 | gǒu | dog | 6 |

H

| 花瓶 | huāpíng | vase | 1 |
| 划船 | huá chuán | boating | 4 |

J

| 饺子 | jiǎozi | dumpling | 3 |

K

| 烤鸭 | kǎoyā | roast duck | 3 |
| 筷子 | kuàizi | chopsticks | 2 |

M

马	mǎ	horse	6
芒果	mángguǒ	mango	5
门	mén	door	1

N

你好	nǐ hǎo	hello	1
柠檬	níngméng	lemon	5
牛	niú	cow	6

P

爬山	pá shān	mountain climbing	4
盘子	pánzi	plate	2
跑步	pǎo bù	run	4
漂亮	piàoliang	beautiful	1
葡萄	pútao	grape	5

Q

| 骑车 | qí chē | cycle | 4 |

S

| 勺子 | sháozi | spoon | 2 |
| 少 | shǎo | few | 2 |

T

| 跳舞 | tiào wǔ | dance | 4 |

| 兔子 | tùzi | rabbit | 6 |

W

碗	wǎn	bowl	2
尾巴	wěiba	tail	6
我	wǒ	I	5
我们	wǒmen	we	4

X

| 喜欢 | xǐhuan | like | 5 |

Y

| 有 | yǒu | have | 6 |

Z

这是	zhè shì	this is	3
真	zhēn	real	1
猪	zhū	pig	6